Minerals and Rocks

Harcourt

SCHOOL PUBLISHERS

Orlando   Austin   New York   San Diego   Toronto   London

Visit *The Learning Site!*

www.harcourtschool.com

What Are Minerals and Rocks?

A **mineral** is a solid object formed in nature. A mineral has never been alive. Gold is a mineral.

A **rock** is a solid object that forms naturally.
It is made up of one or more minerals.
Granite is a rock made of several minerals.

READING FOCUS SKILL

MAIN IDEA AND DETAILS

The **main idea** is what the text is mostly about. **Details** tell more about the main idea. Look for **details** about minerals and rocks.

Minerals

Did you know that salt is a mineral? A **mineral** is a solid object formed in nature that has never been alive.

No two minerals are exactly alike. Gold is a shiny mineral. Graphite is a dull and dark mineral. It is so soft you can write with it. Diamonds are hard enough to cut steel.

Gold

Graphite

Halite

Minerals are used in many ways. Quartz can be used to make glass for windows. Diamonds and gold are used in jewelry. Iron comes from minerals and is used in buildings. Copper used in pennies before 1983 came from minerals.

What are three ways minerals are used?

Garnet

Mica

Quartz

Ways to Identify Minerals

There are many ways to identify minerals. One way is to use color. Some minerals are one color. Others can have more than one color. Quartz can be pink, purple, white, or black.

You can also identify minerals by how hard they are. The scale below is used to tell the hardness of minerals. The hardest mineral is 10. The softest mineral is 1.

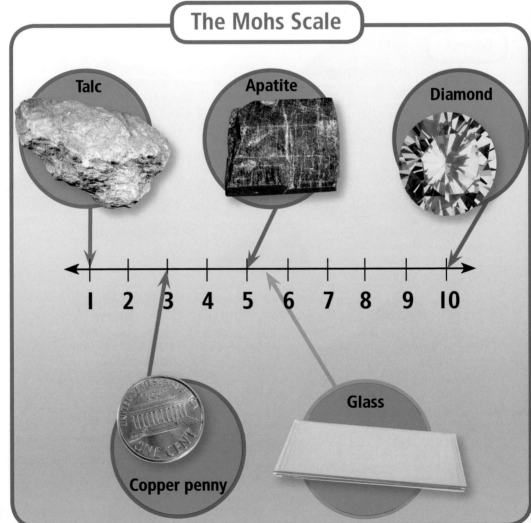

The Mohs Scale

Talc

Apatite

Diamond

1 2 3 4 5 6 7 8 9 10

Copper penny

Glass

When you rub a mineral against a rough white tile, it leaves a streak. *Streak* is the color of the powder left behind. Streak is another way to identify a mineral.

 Tell three ways to identify a mineral.

▼ Making a streak.

Rocks

Rocks make up most of Earth. A **rock** is a solid made of one or more minerals. Rocks form naturally.

Granite is a rock. It is made of several minerals. Granite is very strong, so many buildings are made of granite.

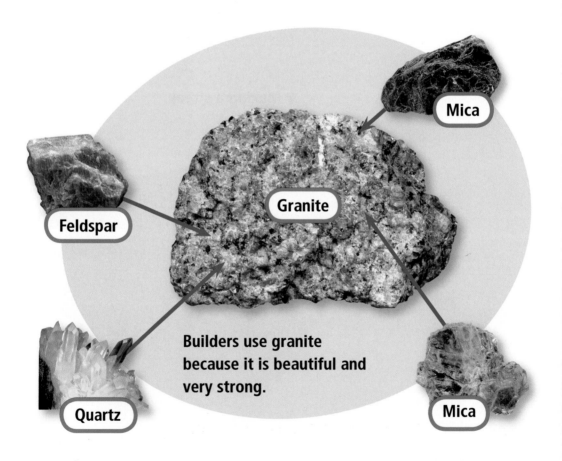

Mica

Feldspar

Granite

Quartz

Builders use granite because it is beautiful and very strong.

Mica

Earth has three main layers. You live on the outside layer. It is called the crust. Below the crust is the mantle. The core is the center of Earth.

 Tell what makes up rock.

Earth's layers ▶

Crust

Mantle

Core

Review

 Complete this main idea statement.

1. Earth is made mostly of _____.

Complete these detail sentences.

2. Rocks are made up of one or more _____.

3. Minerals are _____ objects formed in nature that were never alive.

4. Color, hardness, and _____ are ways to tell one mineral from another.

VOCABULARY

igneous rock
sedimentary
rock
metamorphic
rock

What Are the Types of Rocks?

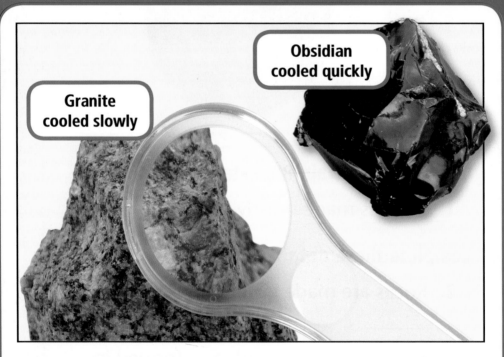

Granite
cooled slowly

Obsidian
cooled quickly

Igneous rock was once melted rock. It then cooled and hardened. Igneous rock that cooled quickly looks like glass. Igneous rock that cooled slowly has large grains.

Limestone

Sedimentary rock is made from materials that settle into layers. The layers are squeezed until they form rock.

Gneiss

Metamorphic rock is rock that has been changed by heat and pressure. Gneiss (NYS) is a metamorphic rock.

When you **compare and contrast**, you tell how things are alike and different.

Look for ways to **compare and contrast** types of rocks and how they form.

Types of Rocks

Rocks are grouped by how they form. There are three main types of rocks.

Igneous rock was once melted rock. It then cooled and hardened. Some igneous rock cooled quickly. It looks like glass. Some igneous rock cooled slowly. It has large grains.

Igneous Rock

Granite

Obsidian (uhb•SID•ee•uhn)

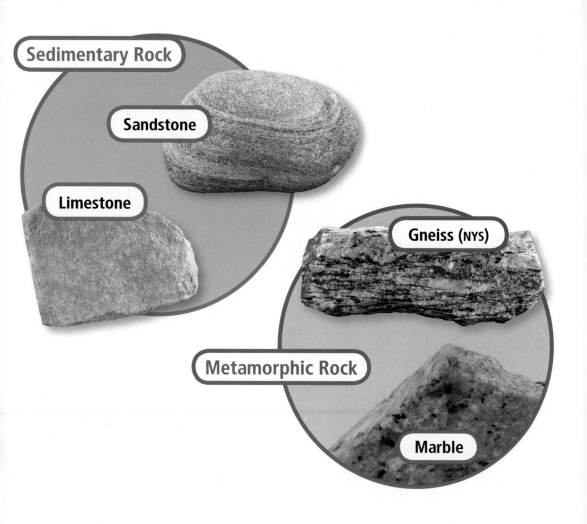

Sedimentary Rock

Sandstone

Limestone

Gneiss (NYS)

Metamorphic Rock

Marble

Sedimentary rock forms from materials that settle in layers. The layers are squeezed together until they form rock.

Metamorphic rock is rock that has been changed by heat and pressure.

Focus Skill **Tell how igneous rock and sedimentary rock are different.**

How Rocks Form

Each kind of rock forms differently. Igneous rock begins as melted rock below Earth's surface. It then rises to the surface through volcanoes. It cools and hardens to become igneous rock.

Sedimentary rock forms when wind and rain break rock into bits and carry it away with soil. The bits settle into layers. Over time, the layers harden into rock.

Melted rock from volcanoes becomes igneous rock. ▼

Layers of rock bits form sedimentary rock. ▼

Metamorphic rock forms in another way. Rock inside Earth is soft from Earth's heat. Pressure in Earth's crust squeezes the rock. There it changes into metamorphic rock.

 Tell how rock forms in different ways.

Soft rock inside Earth becomes metamorphic rock. ▼

The Rock Cycle

Over time, one kind of rock can become another kind. Igneous and metamorphic rock can break down and become sedimentary rock. Any rock that melts and cools can become igneous rock. Any rock in Earth's crust can become metamorphic rock under heat and pressure.

Changing from one kind of rock to another is called the rock cycle. The diagram shows the rock cycle.

How can all rocks change?

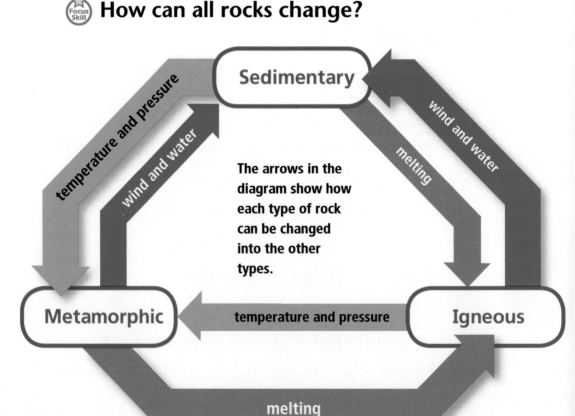

The arrows in the diagram show how each type of rock can be changed into the other types.

How People Use Rocks

People use rocks in many ways. Granite is used to make buildings. Crushed sedimentary rock is used to make bricks. Artists make statues out of marble.

 How are rocks used in different ways?

Mount Rushmore is mostly igneous and metamorphic rock. ▶

Review

Focus Skill

Complete the compare and contrast statements.

1. _____ , sedimentary, and metamorphic rock are formed in different ways.

2. _____ rock is formed by heat and pressure, and _____ rock is formed from layers of material squeezed together.

3. Igneous rock looks like _____ when it cools quickly, but has large _____ when it cools more slowly.

What Are Fossils?

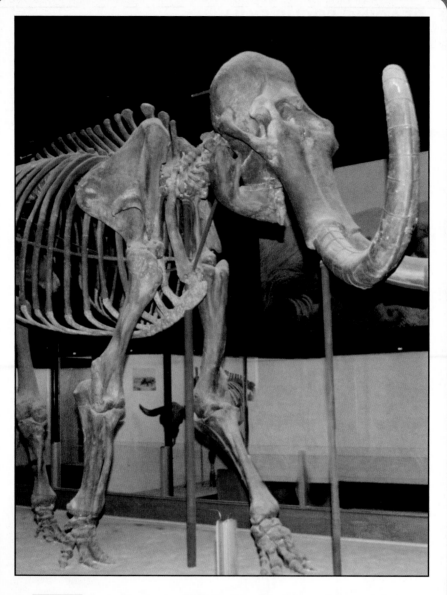

A **fossil** is what is left of a living thing that died a long time ago. Some fossils are bones, teeth, and shells that turned to rock. Other fossils are imprints made in mud made by plants and animals.

READING FOCUS SKILL
MAIN IDEA AND DETAILS

The **main idea** is what the text is mostly about. **Details** tell more about the **main idea**.

Look for **details** about different kinds of fossils.

Fossils

A **fossil** is a mark or the remains of a living thing that died long ago.

There are many kinds of fossils. Some fossils are animal parts, such as shells, bones, and teeth, that have turned to rock over time.

Triceratops fossil ▶

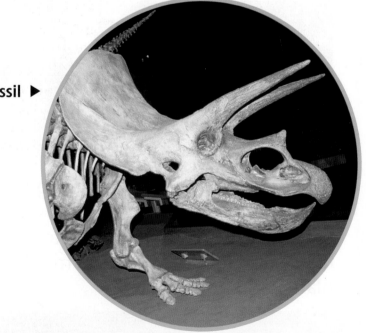

Dinosaur imprints are fossils.

Other fossils are marks left by animals or plants. The marks are called imprints.

Plants and animals make imprints in mud. The mud hardens and changes to a rock. It is now a fossil. Feathers and leaves can make imprints. Footprints in mud can also turn into fossils.

 Tell about the different kinds of fossils.

How Fossils Form

Some fossils began forming millions of years ago. Use this diagram to see how they formed.

 How do fossils form?

1. The soft parts of an animal rot away.

2. The hard parts, such as shells and bones, are covered by mud and sand.

3. Over a long time, the bones, mud, and sand turn to rock.

Learning From Fossils

Fossils are clues. They tell about life on Earth long ago. Scientists look at the shapes of fossil teeth. They compare the teeth to today's animals. This tells them what foods an animal might have eaten. Scientists also use fossils to learn what a place was like long ago. Clam fossils show that a sea once covered the place where the fossils were found.

Scientists dig carefully for fossils.

 Tell what scientists learn from fossils.

Review

 Complete the main idea statement.

1. Fossils tell about _____ and animals that lived long ago.

Complete the detail statements.

2. Some fossils are bones that turned to _____.

3. Some fossils begin as marks left in _____.

4. _____ use fossils to learn about life on Earth long ago.

23

GLOSSARY

fossil (FAHS•uhl) A trace or the remains of a living thing that died a long time ago

igneous rock (IG•nee•uhs RAHK) Rock that once melted but then cooled and hardened

metamorphic rock (met•uh•MAWR•fik RAHK) Rock that has been changed by heat or pressure

mineral (MIN•er•uhl) A solid object found in nature that has never been alive

rock (RAHK) A naturally formed solid made of one or more minerals

sedimentary rock (sed•uh•MEN•ter•ee RAHK) Rock made when materials settle into layers and get squeezed until they harden into rock